Colours of the Alphabet

Volume 2

By Sarah McPherson

Colours of the Alphabet – Volume 2

Written by Sarah McPherson

Copyright © Tarva Publishing

All rights reserved. No part of this book may be reproduced in any manner whatsoever without prior written permission of the publisher.

First Printing, 2022

Published by Tarva Publishing
www.tarvapublishing.com.au

ISBN 978-0-6454104-9-5

To Katie

Thanks for introducing me to more colours

There are many colours of the Alphabet
in that we do agree,

From Almond, Amazon and Amber
to colours like Zaffre

So can you see your favorite
with the A-Z of colour

Or if you had made this book
would you choose another?

A

Acid Green

B

Blue

C

cyan

D

Dark Orange

E

Eggplant

F

Flame

G

Gold (Metallic)

H

Helioptrope

I

Imperial Red

J

Jade

K

Kombu Green

L

Lilac

M

Mango

N

Nickel

O

Orchid

P

Pear

Q

Queen Blue

R

Rose

S

Saffron

T

Teal

u

unmellow yellow

V

volt

W

wisteria

xanthic

Y

Yale Blue

Z

zaffre

So did you see your favorite, colour in our book?

Head back to the start and take another look!

Red, orange, yellow, green, blue, purple, pink, grey, brown, black, indigo, violet,

www.ingramcontent.com/pod-product-compliance
Lightning Source LLC
Chambersburg PA
CBHW040729020526
44107CB00086B/2987